UNBREAKABLE,

Even When Bent

Angeline Wilcox

DEDICATION

This memoir is lovingly dedicated to two extraordinary men who shaped my life in profound and lasting ways.

To my father, *Bishop Robert Lee Johnson, Sr.,* thank you for the wisdom, strength, and faith you poured into my life. Your guidance, prayers, and example taught me how to stand firm even in life's hardest moments. The values you instilled in me continue to guide my path every day. Your love laid the foundation for the woman I have become.

And to my beloved son, *Tyrell Zachariah Brown, Sr.,* your life was a gift that will forever live in my heart. Though your time here was far too short, the love, joy, and light you brought into this world will never be forgotten. You are my motivation, my strength, and the reason this story must be told. Your memory lives on in every page.

This book is written with love, remembrance, and honor, for the legacy you both carry in my heart.

Forever loved.

Forever remembered.

ACKNOWLEDGEMENTS

For the Man Who Helped Me Find My Voice

There are moments in life when God sends someone not to fix you, but to sit with you.

You came into my life when I was still carrying ashes in my hands. When grief was not a chapter behind me, but a language I was still learning to speak. You did not rush me. You did not try to silence my pain. You did not offer empty answers to questions that have none.

You gave me space.

Space to cry without embarrassment.

Space to speak my son's name without discomfort.

Space to be angry.

Space to heal at my own pace.

You understood grief not as something to solve, but something to honor. You knew that loss changes a person, that it reshapes their breathing, their thinking, their trusting. And instead of being intimidated by that, you leaned in.

You listened.

You held my silence without trying to fill it. You reminded me that my story mattered, not just the beautiful parts, but the broken ones too. Especially the broken ones.

When I doubted whether I should reopen wounds to tell this story, you reminded me that scars are proof of survival. When I questioned whether my voice was strong enough, you reminded me that I had already survived what many never could.

You did not try to compete with my grief. You respected it.

You did not try to erase my past. You honored it.

And in doing so, you helped me see that I am more than what happened to me.

This book exists because you believed I was still here for a reason. Because you saw strength where I still saw fragments. Because you understood that telling the truth is not weakness. It is freedom.

Thank you for loving me gently.

Thank you for understanding the weight I carry.

Thank you for reminding me that even after devastation, life can still hold tenderness.

Most of all, thank you for helping me find the courage to speak.

— *With gratitude and love*

For My Firstborn — My Adult Son

To my son,

You made me a mother.

Before I knew what I was doing, before I understood the weight of responsibility, before life had shaped me into the woman I would become, there was you.

We grew up together in many ways. I was learning how to be strong while you were learning how to walk. I was trying to figure out adulthood while teaching you how to tie your shoes. We were both becoming at the same time.

You saw the struggle.

You saw the hustle.

You saw me tired, scared, determined, and sometimes unsure.

But you also saw me fight.

There were seasons when I felt like I was barely holding everything together. Bills stacking up. Relationships unraveling. Grief creeping in. Yet through it all, you kept rising. You carried yourself with a quiet strength that humbled me.

When tragedy struck our family, I worried about you. I worried about what it would do to your heart. I worried about the weight you might try to carry alone. But even in your own grief, you showed courage. You showed depth. You showed a maturity that reminded me that you were no longer a little boy. You were a man navigating pain with dignity.

You have given me a different kind of joy now. The joy of watching you stand on your own two feet. The joy of seeing your decisions, your independence, your growth.

I am proud of the man you are becoming.

Not because you are perfect.

Not because life has been easy.

But because you continue to move forward despite it all.

You are part of my foundation.

You are proof that even in uncertainty, something beautiful can grow.

No matter how old you get, no matter how far life takes you, I will always remember the little boy who made me "Mom" for the very first time.

And I will always love you with that same fierce, unbreakable love.

— *Mom*

For My Mother

To the woman whose hands were never still, my mother.

Some of my earliest memories are of you standing in the kitchen, flour on your apron, grease popping on the stove, curling irons heating beside pots of food meant to feed more than just us. You gave everything you had to your children, to the church, and to anyone who needed you.

You were strong in ways I did not understand when I was younger. I saw the rules. I saw the structure. I saw the discipline. But I did not yet see the pressure you were carrying, the prayers you whispered when no one was looking, and the sacrifices you made so we could survive.

You were building something bigger than yourself. And sometimes in that building, things were heavy. Sometimes we both were.

But through it all, you showed me endurance. You showed me what it looks like to keep going when you are tired. To give when you feel empty. To stand firm when the world presses in.

When my life unraveled, when I became a teenage mother, when my marriage cracked, when grief tried to swallow me whole, you were still there. Maybe not always perfect. Maybe not always knowing what to say. But present.

And presence matters.

You helped shape the resilience in me. The determination. The refusal to quit. Even when we did not always see eye to eye, even when silence sat between us, your strength lived inside of me.

I understand you differently now. As a mother myself, I see the weight you carried. I see how impossible it can feel to protect children from everything. I see how love does not always look soft. Sometimes it looks like survival.

Thank you for doing the best you could with what you had.

Thank you for teaching me how to endure.

Thank you for loving us the only way you knew how.

Because of you, I learned how to stand.

And I am still standing.

— Your daughter

For My Brother — My Pastor

To my brother,

Who has been both shepherd and shield.

Life has taken me through valleys I never imagined walking. Public ones. Painful ones. The kind that test not only your strength, but your faith. And through every chapter, the teenage pregnancy, the broken marriage, the unbearable loss, your love never wavered.

Not once.

You have stood in the pulpit preaching hope while quietly holding your sister together. You have spoken truth with conviction, yet carried me with compassion. You never reduced me to my mistakes. You never defined me by my worst moments. You never let the whispers of others become louder than your loyalty.

You were my pastor, but more importantly, you were my brother.

When my faith felt fractured, you did not condemn me for questioning. When anger at God burned in my chest, you did not shame me for feeling it. You reminded me that even David cried out in confusion, that even Job wrestled with sorrow that even Jesus wept.

You covered me in prayer when I didn't have the strength to pray for myself.

You defended me when I was too tired to defend myself.

You loved me when loving me may not have been easy.

There is something sacred about a love that does not shift with circumstances. A love that does not retreat when life gets messy. A love that stands steady while everything else falls apart.

Yours has been that love.

Thank you for being a constant in a life that has known so much change.

Thank you for protecting my heart when it was exposed.

Thank you for being a pastor who leads with grace, and a brother who loves without conditions.

Because of you, I have seen what unwavering love looks like.

And I will always be grateful.

— *Your sister*

For My Twin — My First Friend

To my twin sister,

Before the world knew us, we knew each other.

We shared a womb. We shared a childhood. We shared secrets whispered in the dark and glances across crowded rooms that said everything without words. There is something sacred about being a twin, a bond that doesn't have to be explained because it simply is.

You have been my mirror and my witness.

You saw me when I was the sheltered girl.

You stood beside me when I became the pregnant teenager.

You walked with me through marriage, separation, and grief.

And on the worst night of my life, you were there. Not by accident, but by grace. When I ran into your room with words I could barely form, you didn't hesitate. You got up. You drove. You held space for my panic and my pain. When my world shattered, you were standing close enough to catch the pieces.

That is what twins do.

You have loved me in silence and in storms. You have known my moods without explanation. You have carried my secrets without judgment. When I doubted myself, you reminded me who I was. When grief tried to swallow me whole, you stayed, not with empty words, but with presence.

There were moments when I didn't have the strength to speak, and you understood anyway. Moments when my tears said more than language ever could, and you did not look away.

You are more than my sister.

You are my built-in friend.

My safe place.

My constant.

No matter how far life stretches us, no matter how different our journeys may look, we are forever connected, by blood, by memory, by survival.

Thank you for loving me without conditions.

Thank you for standing beside me in light and in darkness.

Thank you for being the other half of a bond that grief, distance, and time could never break.

We came into this world together.

And in so many ways, we have walked through it together too.

— *Your twin*

For My Brother

To my brother,

There is something powerful about having someone who has known you your entire life, not just the polished version, not just the survivor, but the little girl you used to be.

You have seen every version of me.

The sheltered child.

The struggling teenager.

The young mother trying to find her way.

The grieving mother fighting to breathe.

And through every season, you remained steady.

You never let my mistakes define me. You never let my pain embarrass you. You never turned your back when life became complicated or messy. Your love didn't shrink when my world fell apart. It expanded.

In moments when I felt exposed, you protected me.

In moments when I felt weak, you reminded me of my strength.

In moments when I wanted to give up, you quietly stood beside me until I found the courage to keep going.

Brothers are often seen as protectors in childhood, but you have been my protector in adulthood too. Not with loud declarations, but with consistency. With presence. With loyalty.

When grief changed me, when loss reshaped my heart, you didn't try to fix me. You simply stayed. And sometimes, staying is the greatest act of love there is.

Thank you for being dependable when so much felt uncertain.

Thank you for loving me without conditions.

Thank you for reminding me that family is not just blood. It is commitment.

No matter what life has taken from me, I have never lost the blessing of having you as my brother.

And that is something I will always be grateful for.

— *Your sister*

ABOUT THE AUTHOR

Angeline Wilcox is an educator, a wife, a mother, and an advocate whose life has been shaped by faith, resilience, and an unwavering commitment to helping others. As a dedicated teacher, she has spent years working with young people, encouraging them to believe in their potential and guiding them toward brighter futures through education.

Angeline's life journey has included both deep joy and profound loss. The tragic loss of her son to gun violence forever changed the course of her life. Rather than allowing grief to silence her, she chose to use her voice to honor his memory and bring awareness to the devastating impact of gun violence on families and communities.

Through her memoir, *Unbreakable, Even When Bent*, Angeline shares a deeply personal story of love, faith, heartbreak, and healing. Her hope is that readers who face their own storms will find strength in her story and be reminded that even in life's most painful moments, it is possible to endure, grow, and remain unbreakable.

Angeline continues to live with purpose, supporting young people, uplifting families, and advocating for change. She believes that every story has the power to heal, inspire, and bring light to others who may be walking through darkness.

She currently lives in Georgia, where she continues her work in education and remains committed to honoring the legacy of her son through advocacy, awareness, and love.

CONTENTS

CHAPTER ONE:

THE WEIGHT OF FAITH AND SILENCE

Some of my earliest memories are filled with the smell of homemade biscuits and hair products.

My mother believed in feeding the entire congregation and keeping their hair done. Our house never smelled like just one thing. It smelled like an old country buffet and a beauty salon sharing the same small space. Grease popping on the stove. Flour dusting the countertops. Curling irons heating up in the kitchen as well. The sweet, thick scent of pressing oil drifting down the hallway.

On Saturdays, women from church would sit at our kitchen table with foil in their hair while pots simmered on the stove. On Sundays, everyone would come to enjoy what simmered on the stove the day before. My mother's hands were always busy, kneading dough, pressing or rodding hair, passing plates, fixing collars.

Revival. Bible study. Choir rehearsal. Women's meetings. Youth nights. Sunday morning and Sunday evening. If the doors were open, we were there. Sometimes I would sit on the pew swinging my legs, staring up at the old stained ceiling, wondering quietly if all of this churching was necessary.

Faith wasn't just something we practiced.

It was the air we breathed.

I didn't know then that air could also feel so heavy.

It shaped what we wore.

What we watched.

Who we spoke to.

Where we went and where we didn't.

God was discussed over breakfast and quoted before bedtime. Scripture corrected behavior faster than any scolding. We didn't just attend church. We belonged to it. It defined our schedule, our friendships, and our reputation.

I loved parts of it. The music that rose and wrapped around the sanctuary. The way voices blended during hymns. The comfort of routine. But I also felt the constant pressure to be good. To be pure. To represent our family well. To never be the reason someone shook their head and said, "What a shame."

To the outside world, we were "that family." The quiet ones. The strict ones. The ones who didn't celebrate certain holidays and didn't allow sleepovers. My parents believed they were protecting us from the world. In many ways, they were trying to. But children at school don't always understand protection. They understand difference.

And different is often lonely.

I remember the whispers first. The giggles behind cupped hands. The questions asked not out of curiosity but as a performance for others.

"Why can't you come to my birthday party?"

"Why do you wear that?"

"Is it true your parents think everyone else is going to hell?"

I didn't have answers that made sense to other children. I barely had answers that made sense to me. I only knew that when I walked into school, I carried something invisible that made me stand out. It was like wearing a sign I couldn't take off.

At recess, I learned how to shrink.

I became smaller in my movements, quieter in my speech. I watched people before deciding where to sit. I laughed when others laughed, even when I didn't understand the joke. I tried to smooth the edges of myself so no one would have anything sharp to grab onto.

But children can sense difference the way dogs sense fear.

The teasing became routine. Sometimes it was words. Sometimes it was exclusion. I learned how to pretend it didn't hurt. I learned how to smile when my stomach felt tight. I learned how to go home and say, "School was fine," because I didn't want to add more weight to my parents' already serious faces.

Home was supposed to be safe.

And in many ways, it was. My parents loved us the only way they knew how, firmly, faithfully, and without apology. But love does not always see what it does not expect. And evil does not always arrive looking like a stranger.

Sometimes it wears a familiar face.

Because my parents devoted so much of their time and energy to building and sustaining the church, their attention was often elsewhere, focused on sermons, congregants, and the endless work of keeping faith alive in others. The house, the community, the gatherings demanded them.

And in that focus, some things went unnoticed. Some things were quietly hidden in plain sight.

I didn't understand it then. I only knew that the world I thought was safe sometimes wasn't. That the person I trusted, my uncle, could hurt me in ways no one saw and in ways no one stopped.

He was family. That's how I understood him. An uncle. A person whose name was spoken casually in conversations. Someone who showed up at gatherings and laughed too loudly. Someone adults trusted.

I didn't have language for what was happening when it first began. Children rarely do. I only knew that something felt wrong. My body would go still, but my mind would float somewhere else, to the songs sung in church, to the birds chirping outside, to the pattern in the rusted tin on the barn walls.

When you are young, you assume adults know what they are doing.

You assume if something bad were truly happening, someone would stop it.

So when no one stopped it, I began to think maybe the bad thing was me.

Shame is a strange thing to hand a child. It doesn't fit in their small palms, but they carry it anyway. I carried it quietly. I carried it to school, where I was already different. I carried it to church, where sermons about purity made my chest tighten. I carried it in the way I avoided eye contact and the way I flinched at sudden touch.

I did not tell.

Not because I didn't want help. But because I didn't know how to explain something I didn't understand myself. Because I was afraid of breaking my family in half. Because when you are already the strange girl at school, the last thing you want is to become something else too.

So I split myself instead.

There was the outside me, obedient daughter, quiet student, polite child who said "Yes, ma'am" and "No, sir." And then there was the inside me, confused, afraid, carrying questions too big for her small body.

- Why me?
- Did I do something wrong?
- If I were better, would this stop?

Children are experts at blaming themselves.

At school, the bullying continued. Sometimes it felt like the universe had decided I would be the easy target everywhere. If it wasn't my family's beliefs, it was my clothes. If it wasn't my clothes, it was my silence. Kids would mimic the way I talked about church. They would exaggerate my seriousness. They would dare each other to ask me questions meant to embarrass.

I began to dread mornings.

But even then, something inside me refused to disappear completely.

I started writing in secret. Small scraps of paper hidden in drawers. Little prayers that didn't sound like the ones spoken at church. Mine were messy and honest.

- "Please make it stop."
- "Please make me normal."
- "Please let someone see me."

I didn't know it then, but that small act, putting words to pain, was the beginning of survival.

There is something powerful about a child who keeps going.

Even when she doesn't understand.

Even when she feels alone.

Even when the world feels unsafe in places it shouldn't.

Looking back now, I wish I could step into that schoolhouse with all the laughing and murmuring. I wish I could kneel in front of that little girl and tell her what she could not yet know:

You are not the shame.

You are not the problem.

You are not what was done to you.

And one day your voice will be louder than your silence.

But in those early years, all I knew was this: I was trying to survive in a world that felt confusing and heavy. I was trying to be good enough for God, quiet enough for school, invisible enough at home.

I did not yet know that surviving was its own kind of strength.

And I did not yet know that telling the truth would one day set me free.

Chapter Two

Fifteen and Showing

I remember the smell first.

Bleach and something floral, trying too hard to be clean. The bathroom was small, the fan humming above me like it knew a secret. I sat on the edge of the tub with a thin white stick trembling in my hand. My heart beat so loudly I was sure someone in the next room could hear it.

I was fifteen years old.

Still sleeping with my sister and a nightlight. Still asking permission to go anywhere, knowing the answer would be no. Still sitting in the youth section at church on Sundays.

I stared at the test, willing it to change. Willing the second line to fade. Willing God to undo whatever had already been done.

It didn't fade.

The silence that followed was heavier than any sermon I had ever heard. I didn't cry at first. I just felt suspended. Like my body was still in that bathroom, but my spirit had stepped outside of it, hovering near the ceiling, watching a little church girl realize her childhood had just ended.

I wasn't rebellious.

I wasn't wild.

I wasn't trying to prove anything.

I was confused.

I was wounded.

And I was carrying shame long before I ever carried a baby.

The Secret

For weeks, I told no one.

Morning sickness became my private battle. I learned how to swallow nausea in the hallway at school. I kept crackers in my pocket. I blamed stomach bugs. I avoided the cafeteria when smells felt too strong.

I started wearing oversized clothes, even though it looked tacky. I folded my arms over my stomach as if I could shield the truth back inside me. Mirrors became enemies. I avoided them whenever possible, in the bathroom, in store windows, at church.

Especially at church.

Every Sunday, I sat in the pew and prayed the same desperate prayer:

Please let this go away.

Please let this not be real.

Please don't let them find out.

But reality does not disappear because a fifteen-year-old is afraid of it.

My body began to change. Slowly at first. Then undeniably.

And secrets always grow heavier before they are exposed.

The Telling

My mother found out first, somehow. I guess it was just a mother's intuition.

I don't remember every word, but I remember her face. The way her eyes scanned mine, searching for something, an explanation, a denial, a different ending. I remember her sitting down as if the air had been knocked out of her.

My father didn't yell. He simply asked if I was pregnant because of a rumor he had heard. Of course, I instantly told him no. I know he didn't believe me, but he never uttered another word about it.

His silence grew, and that hurt me more than him yelling.

He stood still, jaw tight, eyes distant. Disappointment filled the room thicker than anger ever could. I wanted him to shout. I wanted him to say something loud enough to drown out my shame.

Instead, there was quiet.

And in that quiet, I felt smaller than I ever had in my life.

News travels fast in church communities. Faster than forgiveness. Faster than understanding.

Whispers replaced greetings.

People who used to hug me now offered tight smiles. Adults who once called me "such a sweet girl" now looked at me as if I had personally betrayed them.

No one asked if I was scared.

No one asked if I was okay.

They only asked how this could have happened.

As if I were a cautionary tale instead of a child.

Ostracized

I stopped sitting with the youth group.

No one officially told me I couldn't, but space opened around me like an invisible barrier. Conversations hushed when I approached. Girls I had grown up with avoided eye contact.

I heard my name in sentences that didn't include me.

- "She knew better."
- "Her parents raised her better."
- "This is what happens when…"

I became the example.

The lesson.

The warning.

Adults spoke about me instead of to me. Decisions were made for me, prayers were said over me, but very few words were spoken directly into my heart.

I wasn't seen as a girl who was hurting.

I was seen as a girl who had failed.

And shame layered itself over trauma like a second skin.

School Ends

The day I stopped going to school felt unreal. The hallways, the lockers, the laughter of classmates, everything became a world I could no longer inhabit. I was sixteen, and suddenly my life was measured not in homework and friendships, but in diapers, bottles, and sleepless nights.

I had to support my baby. Every choice, every sacrifice felt permanent. My parents already carried more stress than anyone should have to bear, raising four children while trying to keep the church and our home running. I didn't want to add to their burdens, so I carried mine silently.

Childhood was supposed to be mine to live, to explore, to stumble and laugh and dream. But it ended the moment I held my baby in my arms and realized the world expected me to be everything, provider, protector, and mother, all before I even knew who I was.

While my peers went to football games and school dances, I learned how to rock a crying newborn at three in the morning. I learned the rhythm of feeding schedules and exhaustion. I learned how to function on broken sleep and unspoken grief.

And yet, even in that unreal moment, I loved him fiercely. I loved him more than I loved myself. I loved him so much that fear, shame, and exhaustion became background noise to the rhythm of keeping him alive.

It was my anchor. My only certainty. And in that love, I discovered something I had not yet realized: that surviving, even when the world turns against you, is its own kind of strength.

But love does not cancel exhaustion.

Some nights I cried softly so no one would hear. I didn't want to seem ungrateful. I didn't want anyone to think I regretted my child.

I didn't regret my baby.

I grieved my girlhood.

There is a difference.

Becoming

Somewhere between bottles and Bible verses, I stopped being "the church girl."

I became "the teenage mother."

Labels replaced my name.

But something else was forming too, something quiet but strong.

Responsibility.

Resilience.

A kind of love that grows in fire.

I was now sixteen. Still unsure. Still carrying the weight of everyone's opinions. But when I held my baby against my chest, I felt something steady for the first time in months.

They saw my mistake.

They saw my belly.

They saw what they wanted to judge.

But they did not see the courage it took to wake up every day and keep going.

They did not see the fear I swallowed.

They did not see the prayers I whispered over my baby in the dark.

They saw my sin.

They never saw my survival.

CHAPTER THREE

TRYING TO BUILD A FAMILY

I thought love would fix everything.

At sixteen, with a baby on my hip and judgment still clinging to my name, I believed that if I could just build something that looked like a family, the whispers would quiet down. If I could make it “right,” maybe the shame would loosen its grip.

The man everyone believed was my child’s father stood beside me in public. He was the solution people could point to. The explanation that made the story cleaner.

But the truth was more complicated.

And when the truth surfaced, it brought a new layer of humiliation I was not prepared for.

The Secret inside the Secret

At first, everyone assumed he was the father. It fit the narrative. It was convenient. It allowed people to nod and say, “Well, at least they’re trying.”

I let them believe it.

Part of me wanted it to be true, not because of biology, but because it made things simpler. It meant there was a structure. A box I could check. A story that made sense.

But when questions arose, and timelines were counted, and doubt crept in, the reality came crashing down.

He was not the biological father.

The moment that truth came out felt like being exposed all over again.

The same people who had already judged me now had something new to dissect. I wasn't just the pregnant church girl. I was now the confused one. The reckless one. The cautionary tale with extra details.

Shame multiplied.

It wasn't just that I had disappointed my parents. It wasn't just that I had embarrassed the church. Now my story didn't even fit neatly into the version people had tried to tolerate.

And in a small town, in a tight church community, complicated stories don't receive much grace.

They receive gossip.

Wanting It to Work Anyway

Even after the truth surfaced, I stayed.

Part of it was pride. Part of it was fear. Part of it was exhaustion from already being judged once. I couldn't bear the thought of another public unraveling.

If he stayed, maybe it would prove something.

Maybe it would prove I wasn't completely undesirable.

Maybe it would prove someone chose me.

Maybe it would prove I was worth committing to, even with my messy history.

But when the biological truth entered the relationship, something shifted in him too.

Resentment crept in.

Arguments sharpened.

The unspoken question hung in the air during disagreements.

"Why am I even here?"

And sometimes it wasn't unspoken.

Moving In

Before I even packed my bags, I found out I was expecting my second child. I remember sitting on the edge of my bed, staring at the tiny lines on the test, and feeling a rush of everything at once: fear, confusion, love, shame, and exhaustion. I was sixteen when I had my first, and now, barely out of that chaos, my body carried life again. My chest tightened, my stomach roiled, and my mind spun with questions I didn't have answers for.

I knew I had to move out because my mom was very stern when she said to me, "You will not bring another baby into this house."

When I moved in with him, I told myself this was stability. This was maturity. This was fixing what had been broken. I clung to that narrative like a lifeline, even as everything around me threatened to pull me under.

The living space was small. Bills were large. Stress sat at the kitchen table with us every night, as constant as the ticking of the clock. I learned quickly how expensive life is when you are barely old enough to drive. Diapers, rent, utilities, gas, formula. Every dollar had a destination before it even arrived. Every hour of my day had been accounted for before I even woke up.

The emotional tension came first.

"You should be thankful I'm helping."

"I didn't have to do this."

"Most guys wouldn't."

Grateful. That word again. As if I were a charity case instead of a partner. As if my presence required repayment.

Then came the mental strain. Criticism dressed as honesty. Subtle reminders of my past. Digs that reopened wounds I was still trying to close.

"You already messed up once."

"Don't mess this up too."

I began shrinking again. Just like I had as a little girl. Just like I had at church. Familiar. Predictable. Safe in its familiarity, though it hurt.

Physical aggression didn't announce itself dramatically. It slipped in during arguments. A shove. A slammed door. An object thrown too close. Fingers gripping harder than necessary.

And afterward came the apologies. Always apologies. Promises. Tears. Blame shifted. Stress blamed. Circumstances blamed.

And I stayed.

Because I wanted love more than I wanted safety.

Because leaving felt like confirming what everyone already thought about me, that I couldn't get it right.

Repeating Patterns

Looking back, I can see it clearly now. Trauma teaches you to tolerate what you shouldn't. I had already learned to silence discomfort, to carry shame quietly, to shrink myself so the world wouldn't notice the damage inside me.

So when chaos entered my adult life, it didn't feel foreign. It felt familiar.

I thought enduring made me strong. I thought staying proved loyalty. I didn't realize I was repeating patterns I didn't yet have language for.

I was searching for belonging in the same places that had once made me feel small. Places where fear and love had always been tangled, where safety and pain coexisted, where the lessons I had learned as a child had prepared me only to survive, not to thrive.

And yet, through it all, life continued inside me. My second child, a tiny reminder of hope and responsibility, grew day by day, even as the world around me felt unsteady. I clung to that life fiercely because it was mine to protect, even if I hadn't yet learned how to protect myself.

Baby Two Arrives

When my second baby was born, I thought maybe, just maybe, I could finally create the stability I had been chasing for so long. I imagined a home where laughter wasn't overshadowed by fear, where meals were full and warm, where love didn't hurt.

I tried. I really did.

Two weeks after giving birth, I went back to work. Two weeks. My body was barely holding itself together, my mind still foggy with pain and exhaustion, and my heart heavy with the responsibility of two lives depending entirely on me. I thought I had no choice. Bills wouldn't wait. Rent wouldn't wait. Formula, diapers, clothes, utilities. None of it would wait.

But my body wasn't ready. My exhaustion wasn't just physical. It was cumulative, built from years of fear, trauma, and survival. Within days, I had a setback. One wrong step, one ignored ache, one too many sleepless nights, and I ended up in the hospital.

There, under the bright lights and the sterile smell of antiseptic, I realized something terrifying. I couldn't do this alone. Not yet. Not safely. Not without risking everything. And yet I had no one to lean on in a way that didn't carry judgment or shame.

Recovering meant relearning how to care for my own body while also caring for two children. Diapers still needed changing, bottles still needed making, and bills still piled on the table like mountains I could never climb fast enough. I felt the pressure in every bone, every muscle, and every breath.

Mothers find a way. Even when the world feels like it's against them. Even when the odds seem impossible.

And so, in the midst of that chaos, I did things I shouldn't have. Desperate times called for desperate measures. Choices I would later regret, but at the moment they were survival.

I learned that motherhood is not always holy or clean. Sometimes it's raw and messy and frightening. Sometimes it requires bending the rules, the ones the world set, the ones faith set, the ones you set for yourself, just to make sure your children eat, breathe, and survive another day.

And yet, even in those moments of desperation, I loved them fiercely. I loved them enough to push past fear. To keep moving forward. To try, even when I didn't know if I could.

Because survival is what mothers do. Even when it breaks you.

But I was exhausted.

Exhausted from pretending everything was fine.

Exhausted from defending him to others.

Exhausted from defending myself to myself.

I didn't know who I was anymore.

Not the sheltered church girl.

Not just the teenage mother.

Not quite a woman.

Just someone trying desperately to hold a fragile structure together.

The Shift

The turning point wasn't dramatic.

It was quiet.

It was the realization that my children deserved peace more than I deserved the appearance of a family.

It was understanding that belonging built on fear is not belonging at all.

The truth about paternity had already exposed me once. But the truth about the relationship was exposing something deeper.

I was worth more than endurance.

And my children were worth more than instability.

I didn't know how to leave yet.

But for the first time, I began to understand that love should not require bruises, on the body or the spirit.

I had searched for belonging in another person.

Slowly, painfully, I was beginning to understand that belonging would have to start within myself.

CHAPTER FOUR

CRACKS IN THE FOUNDATION

The sad part is, I didn't know how to belong. I found myself belonging to someone else. I didn't fall in love.

I escaped.

After years of living in fear, measuring words, bracing for moods, learning the rhythm of someone else's anger, I met a man who felt different. Calm. Attentive. Interested in rescuing me from what he could clearly see was broken.

And when you've been drowning, you don't question the hand that pulls you out.

We hadn't known each other long. Just a few months. But to me, it felt urgent. Necessary. Like a door God Himself had opened so I could run through it.

Marriage seemed like safety.

Marriage seemed like redemption.

Marriage seemed like a clean page after a messy chapter.

So I said yes.

Not because I knew him deeply.

But because I needed out.

Building on Urgency

The marriage came quickly. Faster than wisdom would advise. I told myself that sometimes love moves fast. That when something is meant to be, it doesn't need years to confirm it.

But urgency is not the same as foundation.

I carried my children into a new household, hopeful that this would finally be the family I had been trying to build all along.

What I didn't fully understand was that I wasn't just marrying a man. I was marrying history. Children from previous relationships. An ex who was not quiet about her presence. Conversations I wasn't part of. Tensions that existed long before I arrived.

Blended families don't blend automatically.

They strain.

They stretch.

They expose insecurities you didn't know you had.

There were schedules to coordinate. Feelings to navigate. Boundaries that felt unclear. And always, the presence of another woman connected to my husband through shared children.

"Baby mama drama," people called it casually.

But living inside it didn't feel casual.

It felt exhausting.

It felt like constantly proving my place in a home that was still figuring out where to put me.

Emotional Strain

I wanted to be the good wife.

Supportive. Understanding. Mature.

I told myself that grown women handle complications gracefully. That jealousy was immature. That insecurity was a personal flaw I needed to fix.

So I swallowed feelings.

I adjusted.

I compromised.

Again.

But blending households magnified everything. Financial strain, emotional tension, communication gaps. There were child support payments, unexpected expenses, and the ongoing cost of trying to make multiple worlds coexist peacefully.

Money was tight.

Stress was constant.

And I was still young, still learning myself, trying to function as if I had all the tools adulthood required.

Alone in Marriage

The loneliness didn't arrive all at once.

It crept in.

Late nights when he was distant.

Phone turned face down.

Energy that shifted without explanation.

You can feel when something is off long before you have proof.

Infidelity doesn't just break trust. It fractures identity. It makes you question your instincts, your worth, your attractiveness, your adequacy.

I had worked so hard to become "wife" instead of "statistic."

And yet here I was again, lying awake beside someone who felt miles away.

I asked questions carefully at first. Calmly. Trying not to sound accusatory.

The answers were dismissive. Defensive. Sometimes convincing enough to quiet my suspicions temporarily.

But truth has a way of surfacing.

And when it did, it didn't explode.

It cracked.

Just like the foundation we had built too quickly.

Amid all this, the one person I had always felt truly loved me, my father, was gone. The man who had shown me tenderness in a house that often felt too loud, too busy, and too critical. The man who had lifted me up when I felt unseen. The one who quietly made space for my voice in a world that silenced me.

His passing left a hollow space I could not fill. The grief added another layer to the weight I carried daily. There was no one to reassure me. No steady hand. No familiar laugh to remind me that someone had my back.

My children needed me.

My marriage demanded me.

The bills never stopped.

And yet, in the quiet moments, I felt utterly, achingly alone.

I learned that love can be lost in many ways. Through absence, through betrayal, through death. And each time it leaves, it exposes you to the raw, unprotected parts of yourself you've spent years hiding.

I had survived trauma, early motherhood, and poverty. But losing the one person who truly saw me left me feeling unmoored in a world already tilted too far toward chaos.

Even in that darkness, I tried to keep moving forward. But the lessons of survival learned as a child, tested as a teen, stretched as a young mother were now being called upon in ways I could never have anticipated.

I had to navigate grief, betrayal, and the overwhelming weight of responsibility all at once.

And yet I did what mothers do.

I kept going.

I kept loving.

I kept surviving.

Staying for Appearances

Divorce had always sounded like failure to me.

Especially in church.

Especially for someone whose story already carried so many chapters of "what went wrong?"

I could hear the whispers before they even began.

"She rushed into it."

"She never learns."

"That's why you don't…"

So I stayed longer than I should have.

Smiled in public.

Held hands in church.

Sat through sermons about covenant and endurance, wondering if endurance meant slowly losing yourself.

There is a difference between fighting for a marriage and fighting to maintain an image.

But when you've spent your life being judged, appearances feel like protection.

I told myself every marriage has rough seasons.

I told myself God hates divorce.

I told myself leaving meant proving everyone right.

But quietly, privately, I began asking a different question.

At what point does staying become self-abandonment?

The Realization

The realization was not dramatic.

It was tired.

Bone-deep tired.

Tired of wondering.

Tired of pretending.

Tired of competing with ghosts of relationships past.

Tired of sleeping beside someone who didn't feel emotionally present.

I had survived abuse.

I had survived shame.

I had survived teenage motherhood.

But surviving is not the same as living.

And I was beginning to understand that staying for appearances would cost me more than leaving ever could.

When the church reaction came again, it was predictable. Some offered quiet support. Others offered scripture without context. A few offered thinly veiled judgment wrapped in "concern."

Divorce, to them, was a spiritual failure.

To me, it was a breaking point.

This time, though, I was not a fifteen-year-old girl hiding in a bathroom.

I was a woman recognizing cracks that could no longer be ignored.

The foundation had been rushed.

Built on urgency instead of healing.

And no amount of pretending could make it steady.

CHAPTER FIVE: SINGLE AGAIN, STRONGER THAN BEFORE

And then the final realization settled in like a stone in my chest. The foundation of our marriage was broken. I could try to patch it. I could try to endure. But nothing I did could fix the cracks that had widened too far, too deep, over too many years.

Separation became inevitable. It wasn't dramatic at first. We simply stopped sharing space the way we had before. The bed grew larger between us, not physically, but emotionally. Nights were spent apart. Decisions were made independently.

The divorce wasn't finalized yet. That paper, that signature, that legal acknowledgment of the life we had built and lost had not yet come. But in the quiet of my living space, with the grandkids now asleep and the silence pressing in, I felt the weight of freedom and fear at the same time. Freedom to protect myself and my children. Fear of the unknown. Fear of the emptiness left behind.

Even in the midst of separation, life demanded endurance. Bills didn't pause. Even though our children were adults, they didn't understand the tension. And I had to carry on, a mother, a grandmother, a survivor, a woman learning to exist on her own terms for the first time in years.

Some days I stumbled. Some nights I cried quietly, not wanting my children or grandchildren to see the cracks in my armor. Some mornings I woke stiff and sore from exhaustion, wondering if I could do this, do it all, and still hold on to myself.

And yet, through every exhaustion, every sacrifice, every tiny victory, I began to feel it. A sense of reclaiming myself. I was learning, slowly, how to be both strong and gentle. How to hold my family fiercely without losing sight of who I was. How to survive, not just endure, but survive with intention.

This was my foundation now. Fractured. Uncertain. But mine to rebuild. And I would. Piece by piece. Day by day. Breath by breath.

Because that is what mothers do. That is what survivors do. That is what I was learning to do. Stand again, even when the ground beneath me felt unstable.

The Slow Return of My Voice

For years, I had adjusted myself to fit other people's expectations.

Church girl.

Teen mother.

Grateful partner.

Good wife.

Each role required silence in certain areas. Tolerance in others. Shrinking when necessary.

Now there was space.

And space can be frightening when you've never had it.

At first, I didn't know what I believed anymore. Not about relationships. Not about faith. Not about myself.

I had followed rules carefully in my early life and still found myself wounded. I had rushed into marriage trying to escape pain and found new pain. I had stayed to protect appearances and nearly lost myself.

So I began asking questions I had once been too afraid to voice.

What do I believe?

What does love actually look like?

Is endurance always holy?

Does God require suffering to prove loyalty?

Those questions felt rebellious at first.

But they also felt honest.

And honesty was something I was finally ready for.

Reclaiming Identity

Slowly, I began to reclaim parts of myself that had been buried.

I laughed more freely.

I set boundaries, awkwardly at first, then firmly.

I stopped explaining myself to people who had already decided who I was.

I realized that being separated did not make me defective.

Being a young mother did not make me irresponsible.

Being abused did not make me weak.

The labels that once defined me began to loosen.

I was not just what had happened to me.

I was becoming who I chose to be next.

A Different Kind of Strength

Strength used to mean enduring.

Now it meant choosing.

Choosing peace over appearance.

Choosing healing over hiding.

Choosing truth over image.

Single again, yes.

But stronger than before, absolutely.

Because this time, I wasn't running from something.

I was building toward something.

Toward stability that didn't depend on a man's mood.

Toward faith that allowed questions.

Toward love that did not require self-erasure.

For the first time in my life, I felt like I was standing on ground I had poured myself.

Not rushed.

Not forced.

Not borrowed.

Mine.

And though I was still tired, still balancing work, motherhood, and healing, I no longer felt lost.

I was no longer the sheltered girl.

No longer the shamed teenager.

No longer the desperate wife.

I was a woman learning her own name.

And this time, I wasn't giving it away.

CHAPTER SIX:
THE CALL NO MOTHER SURVIVES

I had already taken the steps I thought would save me, leaving a marriage that no longer felt safe and carving out a space for myself, my children, and my grandchildren. I was learning to stand on my own, to survive on my own terms, to rebuild a foundation I thought had been lost. But nothing could prepare me for the phone call that would change everything.

It came in the weary hours of the morning, that fragile space between night and dawn when the world feels suspended. I rarely woke in the middle of the night to use the bathroom, but on that particular night something stirred me from sleep.

Half awake, I reached for my phone. The glow of the screen pierced the darkness. Several missed calls. Too many for that hour. My heart began to pound before my mind could form a thought. No one calls repeatedly in the middle of the night with good news.

A quiet dread crept up my spine.

As I sat there on the edge of the bed, trying to steady my hands, another call came through. The phone vibrated in my palm, loud in the silence. For a split second, I considered not answering, as if ignoring it could delay whatever reality waited on the other side.

But I answered.

And the words that followed shattered everything.

"They shot your son."

The room tilted. The air left my lungs in one violent rush. My ears rang, as if the world itself had gone silent. I remember gripping the phone so tightly my fingers ached, trying to hold onto something solid while my entire life cracked open in an instant.

That was the moment before everything changed.

The divorce wasn't even finalized yet. Life was already fragile, already full of tension and uncertainty. And then the voice on the other end of the line spoke words that made time stop.

My son, my baby, my anchor, my reason, was gone. Murdered.

For a moment, I couldn't breathe. My chest tightened so violently I thought it might collapse. My knees buckled. My hands shook as if they had been severed from the rest of me. The world blurred around me. The weight of grief pressed down with a force I had never known.

I held the phone like it was a lifeline, as if somehow, if I gripped it tightly enough, the words could be undone. But they couldn't. Nothing could bring him back. Nothing could fix the emptiness now lodged deep in my chest.

I ran to the other room to wake my sister, who just happened to be visiting from out of state. Even now, I don't believe that was coincidence. I shook her harder than I meant to, my voice trembling, barely forming words.

"They shot him. They shot my baby."

She jumped up, confusion turning into horror in seconds. There was no plan. No clarity. Just urgency. I told her to drive me to the scene. I don't remember grabbing shoes. I don't remember locking the door. I just remember the sound of my own heartbeat pounding in my ears as we rushed into the night.

The drive felt both endless and instantaneous. Streetlights blurred past the windows. I kept whispering, "He's okay. He's okay. He has to be okay." I was bargaining before I even knew the outcome.

When we arrived, I saw flashing lights before I saw anything else. Red and blue cutting through the darkness. My sister hadn't even fully stopped the car before I threw the door open. I jumped out while it was still rolling. I ran.

I don't remember my feet touching the ground properly. I remember stumbling. I remember falling at least once, maybe twice, scraping my hands but not feeling the pain. Nothing hurt except the terror rising in my chest.

And then I saw him.

My son lay lifeless on a porch. Still. Too still.

The world around me faded. The officers. The neighbors. The noise. None of it mattered. I ran to him, praying, pleading, hoping that when I reached him he would move, that he would blink, that he would call out, "Mama."

I dropped to my knees beside him and grabbed his hand. It was cold and heavy. I squeezed it tightly, desperately.

He didn't squeeze back.

And in that moment, I knew.

A sound came out of me that I had never heard before, something between a scream and a sob, something primal and broken. I cried out to God right there on that porch.

"Breathe life into my baby! You've raised the dead before! Do it again! Do it for him!"

I believed with everything in me that if God could open graves in Scripture, He could command breath back into my child's body. I waited for a miracle. I waited for his chest to rise. I waited for his fingers to twitch in mine.

But they didn't.

The night stayed silent.

And in that silence, something inside of me shattered.

The grief came like a tidal wave, but so did the anger. Hot. Immediate. Explosive. I had trusted God. I had prayed. I had survived molestation, teenage pregnancy, abuse, and separation. I had endured humiliation and shame. I had kept my faith when it would have been easier to walk away.

And this was the outcome?

I felt betrayed. Abandoned. Furious.

On that porch, holding my son's hand as it lay still in mine, I didn't feel faith. I felt rage. I felt confusion. I felt a mother's heart breaking in real time.

That was the night I stopped being the same person, the person I had just rediscovered.

The loneliness I had been learning to endure during the separation became a chasm. No spouse to comfort me. No father to steady me. Just me, my living space, the silence, and the echo of a life that had been stolen.

Grief arrived like a storm, uninvited and unstoppable. Anger, disbelief, and guilt tangled together so tightly I couldn't tell one from the other.

How could this happen?

Was I enough?

Could I have done something differently?

The life I had been carefully trying to rebuild, my foundation, my sense of control, my small victories as a mother, grandmother, and woman, shattered in a single moment.

And yet, somewhere beneath the waves of shock and despair, a thread of survival remained. Because that is what mothers do? We breathe. We endure. We carry the unbearable weight of loss, and somehow we keep going.

But no one tells you that surviving a child's death is not like surviving anything else. This grief is different. It is deeper. It is sharper. It is not measured by time or logic. It is a wound that cannot fully heal, only be carried forward.

And on that day I realized something I had never fully understood before. There are losses a mother cannot survive without breaking. There are calls that no mother is ever truly ready to receive.

The days after the call were surreal. I moved through them as if underwater, every sound muffled, every movement slowed. The world continued around me, neighbors chatting, traffic humming, church bells ringing, but I was in a different realm, a place where time had stopped and only loss existed.

Anger surged before I even had time to breathe. Anger at the world. At the injustice. At the people who could take something so precious. Anger at God. At myself. At everyone who had ever let him down. I didn't know which direction to point it, so it bounced around inside me, sharp and relentless, leaving raw edges in my chest.

And then came the guilt. That quiet, insidious whisper that perhaps I could have done more. Perhaps I wasn't enough. Perhaps something I had done, or failed to do, had caused this. Mothers carry guilt like a second heartbeat. It doesn't stop. It doesn't rest.

Amid this storm, the world demanded I function. The other grandchildren needed meals, baths, and bedtime stories. I had to do this for his boys. Bills still came. Life did not pause, and neither could I, no matter how much I wanted to disappear.

Church calls came, some offering prayers, some offering judgment. Some whispered about what could have been prevented, others about "lessons to be learned." Their words felt hollow against the grief that pressed against my ribs, their faith offering nothing tangible for the empty space my son left behind.

In those first months I felt fractured. Every part of me ached. Every part of me wanted to scream. And yet every part of me had to hold together for the grandchildren who had lost their dad.

The child who could no longer speak, laugh, or grow lived in memory, in the photographs, in the stories I told myself over and over to keep the edges from breaking completely.

Sleep became a stranger. Eating became a mechanical task. Crying became a private ritual.

I learned quickly that grief does not heal on a schedule. It is chaotic, unpredictable, and overwhelming, a force that can upend every carefully built routine in an instant.

And in the quiet moments, when the world seemed to fall away, I realized something.

Survival would not look like it had before.

Survival would not mean just keeping a roof over my head or food on the table. Survival would mean carrying this loss while continuing to love, to nurture, and to be present for my living child and the grandchildren still here.

Survival would mean redefining strength in the shadow of heartbreak that no one should ever have to endure.

I discovered, painfully, that grief is not something you recover from. It is something you learn to live with. Something you carry and fold into your every breath until one day you find a way to keep standing.

And that was what I had to do.

Keep standing.

For my child.

For the grandchildren.

For myself.

For the boy who could no longer be held.

Chapter Seven:

Grief Has No Manual

The world expects you to move on. Friends, family, even strangers offer platitudes: "Time heals all wounds." "You have other children to care for." But grief does not follow rules, schedules, or logic. Grief is messy. Grief is loud. Grief is constant. And it has no manual.

At first, I was consumed by anger. Anger at God. Anger at the world. Anger at the people who could allow something so cruel to happen. I had prayed for safety, for protection, for love, and yet here I was, carrying a loss too heavy to name. Every time I closed my eyes, I saw his face, and my heart broke all over again.

Then came the guilt. That quiet, insidious voice that whispered: Was I enough? Did I do something wrong? Could I have saved him? Mothers carry guilt like a shadow. It stretches long and dark, clinging to every thought, every memory, and every choice. I questioned myself relentlessly, replaying the past in endless loops, searching for the moment I could have done something differently.

Church, once a place of sanctuary, felt unbearable. The same voices that had judged me in my youth now whispered again. Their faith, their sermons, their prayers could not reach the emptiness I carried. In the past, I had survived shame and ostracization. Now I was learning to survive grief, and grief had no rules, no compassion, and no shortcuts.

Anniversaries, birthdays, holidays each became minefields. Each memory of him, each milestone I could no longer share, felt like a jagged stone pressed into my chest. I learned to breathe around the pain, to take it one day at a time, to live in the moments that were still mine. But the ache never fully left.

Through it all, I discovered something unexpected: grief does not end love. It transforms it. Loving someone who is no longer here means holding them in your memory, in your stories, and in the choices you make for the children who remain. It means carrying their presence quietly and fiercely in every small act of care and devotion.

I also learned that healing is not linear. There are days you feel almost normal, almost whole. And then there are days when the grief returns like a tidal wave, knocking the wind out of you and leaving you gasping. Some days I could function. Some days I couldn't. And both were valid.

Therapy helped sometimes. Writing helped sometimes. Crying in the dark, whispering his name into the quiet night, helped sometimes. But mostly I learned to survive by simply allowing myself to feel, to acknowledge the anger, the guilt, the sorrow without judgment, and to let it exist alongside the love that had never left me and the life that still needed me to be present.

Grief has no manual. It does not respect timelines or expectations. It does not disappear, fade, or resolve neatly. But it can be carried. And in carrying it, slowly and painfully, you begin to find yourself again. Not the person you were before, but someone new. Someone scarred, yes, but still standing. Someone who has learned that survival is not about returning to life as it was, but about creating a life worth living, even when the world feels unbearable.

I learned, in those long, endless days, that grief is love stretching beyond limits. That it is the proof of what we hold most dear. And that somehow, even in its harshest form, it is a guide, teaching endurance, patience, compassion, and the quiet courage to continue.

Chapter Eight

Who I Became

Looking back, it feels almost unreal.

The girl who hid behind her fears, the one who whispered prayers in a bathroom hoping her secret would disappear, that girl seems like someone else entirely. Fragile. Afraid. Silenced.

And yet she is still inside me. Not weakened, but foundational. She taught me endurance. She taught me that even when the world judges, even when shame settles heavily on your chest, you can still survive.

The Pregnant Teenager

Then came the teenager, fifteen years old, rocking a tiny life in her arms, learning the rhythm of motherhood before she had even learned the rhythm of her own heartbeat. That girl knew fear like few ever do. That girl learned love that demanded sacrifice.

She also learned the first lessons of resilience. That survival is not glamorous, but it is necessary. That love does not erase pain, but it can make pain meaningful.

The Divorced Mother

The woman who walked away from a broken marriage, who navigated blended families and betrayal, who faced financial strain and long nights alone, that woman carries quiet strength. She knows the cost of survival. She knows the courage it takes to choose self-respect over appearances and truth over comfort.

She learned to rebuild. To breathe again. To set boundaries. To claim space that was always hers, even if the world tried to dictate otherwise.

The Loss That Shaped Me

And then there was the unthinkable loss, the grief that reshaped the heart and tested every measure of strength I thought I possessed. Losing my son was not a failure. It was not punishment. It was life's cruel reminder that love and loss often walk hand in hand.

Through that devastation, I learned a new kind of resilience. Not the kind forged in survival of shame or abuse, but the kind forged in the quiet commitment to keep living, to keep loving, and to honor the life of someone who will never return.

Realizing I Am Still Here

Through every trial, every heartbreak, every moment when I felt like the weight of the world might crush me, I am still here.

I am still breathing.

I am still moving forward.

I am still finding ways to honor the past without letting it define the present.

And that is my victory. Not the absence of pain, not the perfect life, but the ability to endure, to stand, and to reclaim my voice.

Finding Purpose in My Story

I tell this story not for pity. Not for judgment. Not for accolades.

I tell it so that others may know: survival is not weakness. Endurance is not a crime. Strength is born from struggle.

To the girl hiding in the bathroom.

To the teenager rocking a newborn.

To the woman learning to leave.

To the mother grieving the unthinkable.

You are not invisible. You are not powerless. You are still here.

And being here, in itself, is enough.

I am who I became because of everything I survived.

Not despite it.

Because survival is strength.

Because telling the story is power.

And because, even in darkness, light remains. The light of memory. The light of love. The light of enduring.

I am still here.

And I will keep being here.

Final Chapter
Still Standing

If you are reading this, know this first: *your story matters.* Every scar, every tear, every moment you thought no one could understand, it matters. Your life is not defined by what was done to you, or what you lost, or how the world labeled you. Your life is defined by the courage it takes to keep living, to keep showing up, and to keep believing in yourself.

To the young girls who feel trapped in shame or fear: I see you. I see the girl who hides secrets in bathrooms. I see the girl who prays desperately for her mistakes to disappear. I see the girl who wants love more than safety. Your worth is not measured by the whispers of others. You are enough. You are capable. And you can survive.

To the mothers who have buried children: I see you too. I see the hollow spaces in your days, the nights when grief feels endless, the questions with no answers. I know the unbearable weight of loving someone whose life was stolen too soon. Your pain is shared across time, across hearts, across lives. You are not alone. And while nothing can undo what happened, there is power in living on, in carrying love, memory, and legacy forward.

To church communities and communities everywhere: I speak to you as well. Compassion is more powerful than judgment. Listening is more healing than sermons. Love is stronger than shame. The children, the mothers, the survivors in your midst need understanding more than they need correction. Your words can wound or they can lift. Choose to lift.

Life is messy, and unfair. Life can break you in ways you never imagined.

But here is the truth: surviving does not mean you are weak. Surviving does not mean you are incomplete. Surviving means you have already shown courage beyond measure.

I know pain. I know shame. I know loss. I know grief.

But I also know something even stronger: resilience.

I know the girl who hid behind white curtains.

I know the teenager who rocked a newborn through exhaustion and fear.

I know the young woman who walked away from betrayal and toxic love.

I know the mother who grieved a child taken too soon.

And I am still here.

I was a sheltered girl.

I was a pregnant teenager.

I was a divorced woman.

I was a grieving mother.

And still, I am here.

Still standing.

Still breathing.

Still believing in the possibility of hope.

Still telling my story.

Still living.

And so are you.

Made in the USA
Coppell, TX
16 June 2026

81391395R00043